ASAFO!

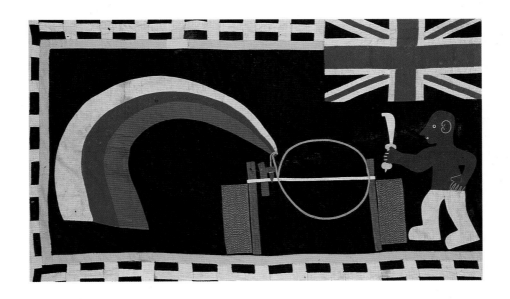

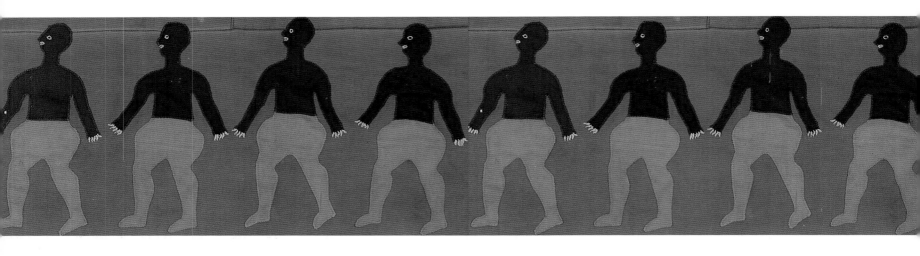

Peter Adler and Nicholas Barnard

Flags selected by Peter Adler and photographed by Ian Skelton

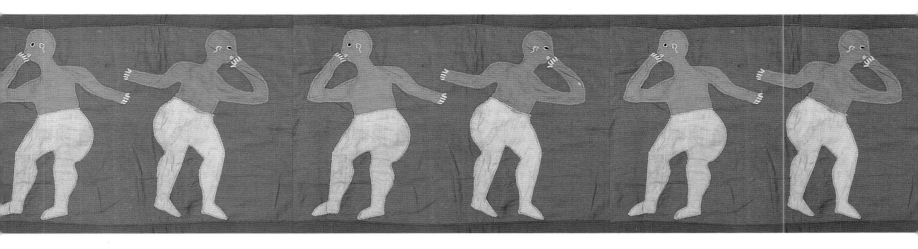

ASAFO !

AFRICAN FLAGS OF THE FANTE

THAMES AND HUDSON

© 1992 Thames and Hudson Ltd, London

First published in the United States in 1992 by
Thames and Hudson Inc., 500 Fifth Avenue,
New York, New York 10110

Library of Congress Catalog Card Number
92-70869

Printed and bound in Hong Kong by Everbest

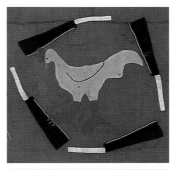

CONTENTS

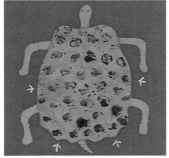

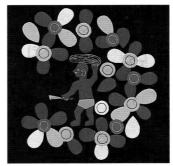

PREFACE

Selecting the flags and close-ups for this book has not been easy. There are many wonderful flags in collections throughout Europe and the United States, and grateful thanks go to all those who kindly gave access to their collections – especially the Chang Trust, Marvin Chasen, Asher Eskanasy, Seymour Lazar, Pierre Loos and Judith Nash. Apologies to those whose flags have not been included.

We are indebted to everyone in Ghana who generously gave so much time, assistance and valuable information – especially Nathan Austin of XYZ Hospitality, George Buzby and family, Yaw Denteh, Ouedraogo Baba Mahama, and all the officers and flagmakers of the Fante Asafo Companies.

Ian Skelton expertly photographed the flags in his London studio with painstaking forbearance and good humour, ably assisted by Vanessa Ballard, Bill Chafty, Milly Donaghy, Karen Onell and Bill Tizzard. To all, our appreciation and thanks.

For their support, advice and assistance, our gratitude goes to Nicholas Calloway, Johnny Carmichael, Maureen Docherty, David Elliott, Lisa Gee, Nathalie Hambro, Regina Ianson, Tom Maschler, Issey Miyake, Kate Moore, Claudia Navone, George Preston and Julian Rothenstein.

Finally, and most importantly, we would like to acknowledge our great debt to Doran Ross for his pioneering fieldwork and essays on the arts and culture of the Fante Asafo. We have heavily relied on his monograph 'Fighting with Art: Appliquéd Flags of the Fante Asafo', published by the UCLA Fowler Museum of Cultural History (1979). For his enthusiastic support and generosity in supplying so much vital information, we offer our grateful thanks.

PETER ADLER and NICHOLAS BARNARD

1

2

INTRODUCTION

This is a book devoted to the celebration of a wonderfully graphic and kinetic tribal art form. From out of West Africa, a land normally associated by the Westerner with the most severe of the tribal arts – with expressive masking and silent statuary – there is to be found a collection of brightly coloured and patterned cloth flags that adorn villages and towns at the time of festivals and funerals. Whether held aloft in a dance, or displayed as banners, the textiles glow with colour, inspire with imagery and excite with allegory. These are the appliqué patchwork and embroidered flags of the Fante people of Ghana.

Today there are over a million Fante people inhabiting the coastal and forest fringes of Ghana, a zone that witnessed the earliest forays of the white man south of the Sahara. The first visitors were a band of Portuguese adventurers who in 1471 sailed along the West African coast on a quest for exotic tradestuffs. From the moment that their ships dropped anchor the culture of the Fante was never to be the same again.

A panoply of Europeans followed the Portuguese. Dutch, French, Swedes, Danes, Brandenburgers and British traded gold, ivory and slaves from within a string of coastal forts for over three and a half centuries. The Fante not only formed strategic alliances with these Europeans to parry the power of the mighty Ashanti Empire, but were also deeply impressed by the technology and by the pomp and pageantry of the 'Oburinfo' ('the people from the hole in the seas horizon').

Such influences were keenly absorbed by the warrior groups of the Fante, known as 'Asafo'. As European military organization was adopted, so the identity of an Asafo company was developed and refined by way of new uniforms, flags and banners. Such a mixture of cultures brought forth an unlikely result, for the Fante craftsmen took to the format of the European flags and created an exuberant art form that marries the ancient West African tradition of communication by proverb with a powerful military display of ceremony and provocation.

The confidence and skill with which the flagmakers have created these visual messages, as well as the wide range of expressive styles employed, is evidence of an extraordinarily vital and exciting graphic art movement that continues to create to this day the flags of the Fante Asafo.

The military institution of the Akan peoples of West Africa, known as 'Asafo', has as its primary role the defence of the state. 'Asafo' sounds

3

4

7

fiercesome when uttered with intent and it is no surprise to learn, therefore, that the derivation of the word is the expressive 'war (sa) people (fo)'. Although these warrior groups are active throughout the Akan area, it is the Fante tribe, inhabiting the coastal region of Ghana, that has developed a sophisticated and expressive community with a social and political organization based on martial principles, and elaborate traditions of visual art.

It is certain that the local organization of warriors into units of fighting men was an established practice well before the arrival of Europeans. Nevertheless, the influence on – and the manipulation of – these groups to suit the trading and colonial ambitions of the foreigners has created many of the qualities of the Fante Asafo that continue to this day.

The situation throughout the Fante region is fraught with political complexities, for there are twenty-four traditional states along an eighty-mile stretch of the Atlantic coast, and each state is independently ruled by a paramount chief ('omanhen'), supported by elders and a hierarchy of divisional, town and village chiefs. In any one state there may be from two to fourteen Asafo companies, with as many as seven active companies in a single town. There is a lack of political unity within the Fante culture as a whole, so that inter-company rivalries – as well as disagreements between the states – are, not surprisingly, endemic. When the Fante were not fighting together against a common enemy, these antagonisms often extended to open conflict among themselves. Observers report that battles between Asafo companies in the eighteenth and nineteenth centuries left many dead and wounded.

By exploiting these divisions, the Europeans could 'divide and rule' and ensure that their control of the coast went unchallenged. At the same time, by organizing the Asafo warriors into efficient military units, they could bring together an army for a quick reaction to any threat from the interior. The enemy was, more often than not, the powerful Ashanti kingdom, a traditional opponent of the Fante, and a dangerous and unpredictable supplier of gold and slaves to the European traders on the coast.

The Asafo companies have been guided in their organizational structure by the direct involvement of the Europeans from at least the seventeenth century. The leader of the combined companies of a single state is a 'tufohen' or general. Each company then has its own commanding officers ('supi'), company captains ('asafohen'), a variety of

5

6

8

lesser officers, flag carriers, drummers, horn blowers and priests or priestesses. Some companies also have a women's auxiliary headed by one or two female officers.

Other European military traditions were adopted by the Asafo, including musketry salutes, marching in procession, the use of distinctive flags and the numbering and naming of companies. Each group is described by a number, a special name, and its town of domicile – for example, 'No.6 Company, Kyirem, Anomabu', or 'No.5 Company, Bromfumba [white man's children], Cape Coast'.

The primary function of the Asafo, as we have seen, was defence of the state. Nevertheless, the companies are key players in a balance-of-power struggle – typical of the many that exist in communities the world over – between the military and civilian groups within government. Although the Asafo are subordinate to their chiefs and paramount chief, they are intimately involved in the selection of the chief and are responsible for his crowning ('enstoolment'). As long as the chief has the support of the people – as represented by the Asafo – he has the authority accorded to him by tradition; the prerogative to appoint and remove chiefs remains with the people. Asafo elders also serve as advisers to the chief.

While Fante chieftaincy is aristocratic and matrilineal – the chief tracing his descent through females back to the founders of the community – the Asafo are patrilineal and democratic. Every child, male or female, automatically enters his father's company, and membership is open to all classes, from stool holders to fishermen.

The Asafo companies are not only the democratic armies of – and political advisers to – the Fante states; they also act, and have acted in the past, as philanthropic social and cultural groups. Sanitation projects and roadworks were their responsibility. State gods came under their protection and they were empowered to conduct the funeral rites for an Asafo member. Local policing was a prerogative. J.C. De Graft Johnson, himself from Cape Coast, commented: 'the Asafu in normal times may be called upon without any previous notice to enter the forest or wood in order to capture a murderer or a highway robber, or to search for a would-be suicide, or to hunt and kill any wild ravaging animal which has become a menace to the community.' Community entertainment, including processions, drumming, singing and dancing at special events, falls within their realm. The companies are justly famous throughout the

7

8

region for their gatherings, such as the annual Akwambo festival (the clearing of the paths to the shrines of titular deities), complete with the colourful costuming, masking, drumming and musical effects that accompany the procession, display and dance of flags in the vicinity of the company shrines.

Of all the sparring, fighting and games-playing units of men worldwide, whether teams of sportsmen and their supporters, formal armies or street gangs, the Fante Asafo take the concept of fighting for and with their art to the height of vernacular expression. At the disposal of each Asafo, there is a wonderfully vibrant mix of art forms with which to remonstrate against an opposing company. Although these include uniforms, sculpture, decorated shrines, banners and dance flags, it is the flags that so perfectly represent the historical temperament of the Asafo.

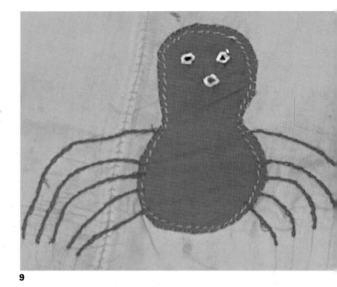

9

The most enduring art forms of the companies are their shrines, the painted cement 'posuban'. Many of them stand sentinel as a house decorated with fantastic figures and monsters, or – shaped as an aggressive painted warship – sail amidst the houses of a Fante village. The flags are the kinetic counterpart to the posuban and also form the most powerful and unifying expression of Asafo creativity.

All the flags that are illustrated within this book are the work of Fante flagmakers active within the last one hundred and twenty years. Whereas the stimulus for their production may be traced to the multivarious European influences from the fifteenth century, the brilliant powers of interpretation and imaginative imagery present in all the flags are quintessentially and uniquely Fante.

The correlation between European interference in the area and the emergence of heraldic flags and banners is clear. It is accepted that the Fante word for a flag, 'frankaa', is a corruption either of the English, or of the Dutch 'vlaggen'. It is not hard to imagine the pomp and ceremony associated with the arrival and establishment of successive European forces and traders. What a fantastic and creatively provocative sight it must have been to witness the coats of arms, national flags and naval ensigns, the logos of trading companies, regimental colours and other military regalia of the visiting and stockading Europeans.

From the contemporary reports and journals of traders and colonialists, we can be certain that Fante flags of local design go back at least until the seventeenth century. In 1693 Phillips, an English trader on the Gold Coast, visited the Akwamu general who had captured Christiansborg

10

Castle from the Danes, and observed: 'The flag he was flying was white with a black man painted in the middle brandishing a scymitar.' In 1706 the Dutch Director-General Nuyts of Elmina wrote of 'fighting men . . . going on a military expedition along the coast in more than eighty canoes with flags and banners flying'. And in 1853 Cruickshank notes that each company has a distinctive flag; for a company member, 'the honour of his flag is the first consideration'. He also comments that some flags are specifically designed as challenges or insults to rival companies.

These visual insults and provocations often resulted in fatal inter-company clashes, in turn leading to the strict control of flag imagery. At Cape Coast, beginning in the 1860s, all companies were ordered to submit their flags to the Colonial Governor for his approval and to register the approved designs and colours with his secretary. The display of unregistered flags was punishable by law. Even today a new flag must be approved by the paramount chief, the general of the combined companies and the Asafo elders, then paraded before all the other companies in the area to make sure that no one is offended.

Fante flags are all approximately three feet by five feet in dimensions. They are made of patchwork from European trade cloth and the material is usually cotton, though silks, satins and felt are also used. The designs and images are appliquéd and occasionally embroidered. Texture and detail are added with chain-stitch embroidery and the use of patterned material. Solid blocks of colour predominate, with as many as fifteen different colours used on a single flag. Each side of the flag shows a mirror image; as a result, the depiction of the company number tends to be confused on one face of the flag or the other. On most flags, all but the hoist side is decorated with borders of repeating triangular and rectangular geometric patterns of alternating colours, and a white cloth fringe is added.

In this selection of old flags, the British Union Jack (or variations of it) is found in the canton; after independence in March 1957, the Ghanaian tricolour replaced the colonial symbol. The transition provides a useful approximate dating mark. It is clear, however, that Asafo companies continued, and continue to this day, to commission flags complete with the British zephyr, to be made for use as direct copies of worn-out old examples.

More prosperous Asafo groups own appliquéd banners of tremendous size. Up to 300 feet long and not much deeper than a dance flag, these banners depict 30 or more distinct images. At festivals the banners are

11

12

displayed full length on wooden poles, leading from the posuban down a main street. Snake- and river-like processions of these banners within the towns or across the adjacent open fields are a dynamic sight indeed.

The installation of a new Asafo captain is the principal motivation for the creation of a flag. It is the responsibility of the incumbent to commission and pay for the ensign, which then becomes the collective property of his company. The choice of design is his, albeit partly limited to mimicking the examples established by precedent to be the artistic property of the company. The personalizing of flags in memory of the commissioning officer is now a common occurrence.

The display of Asafo flags is associated with the social activities of the company and the town as a whole. For the town the major event of the year is the Akwambo (path-clearing) festival. This is a time of unity, of renewing allegiances and friendships and of the homecoming of family members especially for the celebrations. Paths are cleared to shrines of the gods, often by the river, and as this is a large-scale event it is the time of the presentation of new Asafo leaders, such as supi or asafohen. Bearing their flags, the Asafo companies parade through the streets, to the river, to the town shrines and past the houses of the chiefs to demonstrate their allegiances.

At these festivals the companies of a town proudly and aggressively defend the right to parade specific and exclusive colours, cloth patterns, emblems and motifs on their art forms. The violation by mimickry of a company's artistic property, established by precedent and since 1859 by local law, is seen as an act of open aggression.

The flags are also shown at other Asafo events, including the funeral of a company member and the commissioning of a new or remodelled shrine, or on an important anniversary of its original construction. Town, regional and national events, such as the enstoolment of chiefs, the annual Yam Festival and state holidays, are all celebrated with a show of Asafo flags.

At these social events the flags are displayed in a variety of ways. The flagpoles of the posubans, the shrines of each company, proudly carry the flags aloft and the houses of Asafo members adjacent to the shrine, as well as the shrine itself, are decked with strings of colourful colonial and Ghanaian ensigns. Flags are carried in processions and, most dynamically, there is a spectacular display of elaborate dancing with the flag by specially trained Asafo officers, the 'frankakitsanyi'.

13

14

Each company has a dancing corps of four or five members structured in seniority by age, although only one dancer performs at a time, displaying a single flag. The choreography is complex and links all the Asafo military themes of aggression, protection, respect, wisdom and leadership. Supported by the guards of the flag armed with muskets (the 'asikamafu') and the band of drums, trumpets and gong-gongs, the victorious battle scenes of the company are enacted before the other groups of the town. The content of the play is not only associated with the military supremacy of the company; there is considerable entertainment value alone in the rhythm and the athletic skills of many of the dancers.

A flag dancer is apprenticed from the age of eight or ten, spending five or more years living and working as a fee-paying student with the family of his teacher and master. Such training extends to religious studies, for the flag dancers are held to own supernatural powers.

15

No matter how childlike, decorative or abstract the images seem to Western eyes, the Asafo flags are expressively instructive to the Fante. Twinning a proverb with a visual image is central to all Akan art, and to Asafo flags in particular. Akan society had no history of the written word, and so religious, ethical and social codes – as well as law and education – were handed down, maintained and reinforced by this rich and complex oral tradition.

Among the Akan, several thousand proverbs and aphorisms have been documented, though only around two hundred are used consistently in Asafo flag imagery. This limited visual vocabulary is understood throughout the Fante area and allows different groups to 'read' each others' messages.

Although the range of flag imagery is enormous, the principal theme is nearly always the power and glory of the company, usually expressed at the expense of a rival. These deliberately provocative images fall into three categories.

Important historical events, such as a famous company victory in battle, are depicted (61, 62, 67). Such images bolster company pride and also antagonize and intimidate the opposition.

The second category simply identifies the company with an animal, mythological or European image of power and strength. 'After the leopard

16

there is no other' tells rivals that 'leopard' company is the strongest around (142, 147). 'Like the aeroplane, we can go anywhere' (74, 75) identifies the company with that impressive piece of European technology; and with the terrifying image of a multi-headed and winged mythological monster with claws, forked tongue and lethal tail (154–6), the company taunts its rivals with the question, 'Will you fly or will you vanish?' (either way you can't escape us).

The final category is certainly the largest and most complex, and uses a wide variety of proverbs to provoke and challenge with taunts, boasts and threats. Each company, as already mentioned, identifies with specific images of power. 'A dead lion is greater than a living leopard' warns its rival that 'lion' company at its worst is superior to 'leopard' company at its best. 'Although the elephant is stronger, it is the antelope that receives the stool' (rules the forest). Here, a small company identifies with the intelligence of the antelope to counter the power of a stronger opponent. These proverbial challenges also take the form of boasts – 'No one can defeat us except God' (49); insults – 'We came to fight but not you vultures' (102); and warnings – 'It is a foolish mouse that steals from the bag of the cat' (84, 138).

An elephant with its trunk around a palm tree is a very common Asafo image and was used by Britain as its symbol for the Gold Coast colony (183). This one image has three quite separate interpretations. An 'elephant' company will say, 'Only the elephant can pull down the palm tree' (considered the strongest tree and a Fante symbol for eternity). A company identifying with the tree will say, 'Even the elephant is unable to uproot the palm tree'. And there is even (unusually) a compromise interpretation: 'Unable to defeat the palm tree, the elephant made friends with it.'

In spite of the militant nature of much Asafo imagery, many educational and social values are expressed as well. 'The monkey leaps only as far as it can reach' (134–6, 186) not only warns opponents not to attempt what is beyond them, but also advises a child to 'Look before you leap' or 'Don't bite off more than you can chew.' 'Without the head, the snake is nothing but rope' certainly insults the 'snake' company, but it also stresses the importance of strong leadership in the community.

17 'A good spirit always looks after her young', that is, protects the company. (See also 52)

18

19

20

MAN AND MAN

21

22

23

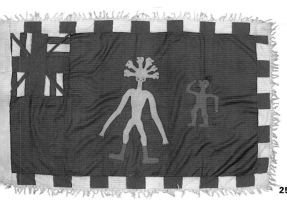

25

26

In this section the Fante community is depicted both at peace and at war. Scenes of domestic and village life (30–8, 175, 200) move to images of violence and conflict (23, 28, 57–67, 201). The Fante world was constantly under threat, both from within and from their powerful northern neighbours, the Ashanti. The Asafo realized that in this situation, European technology, and not the ritual power of chiefs, was the trump card. It is no wonder, then, that they identified so strongly with European might.

These symbols usually lack the rich proverbial associations of local images and simply identify the company with European power. 'The train is always ready to go' (29, 76, 77), 'The ship can carry a load of any size' (72, 73). Locks and keys in the hands of Europeans kept people in or out of an area, bringing freedom or slavery, and so their power was very real. The Asafo say, 'We are the lock and key of the State' (174). Thirty European forts along the Fante coastline were impressive symbols of defensive strength (18, 70, 71, 184). Muskets, rifles and cannons equalled 'firepower' (22, 26, 63, 65, 67, 71), and the draughtboard was used as a visual metaphor for war and to challenge rival companies (68, 69, 91).

Marching men elicit the proverb, 'We come in peace but are always prepared for war' (53–6), and a more provocative image

is that of one company catching another in a fishing net (66). Such an image brandished by No.4 Company Elmina before No.1 Company at a festival in July 1991 nearly caused a riot.

Dwarves and giants also have their place in the corpus of flag imagery. Dwarves are held to have powers of communication with the spirit world and so are placed on a flag as storyteller or as the linguist for a fantastic creature. More amusing is the image of a striding giant bearing on his head a barn full of grain or people (39). The Asafo companies' desire to show the limitlessness of their strengths and powers certainly knows few boundaries. Such feats of the impossible are shown by men carrying absurdly heavy loads (like the world or an elephant) on their heads (43, 44, 139), or by the image that elicits the proverb, 'We can carry water in a basket using a cactus as a cushion' (129). Although Christianity is now the dominant religion, the ancient traditional beliefs in ghosts, ancestors, bush spirits and monsters still survive (17, 50–2, 106, 107, 152–6, 176, 181). One of the most powerful and haunting images in this book is that of a multi-headed bush spirit suckling her young (52). By coming under her protection, a supernatural ally is added to the company's arsenal, and enemies are warned, 'A good spirit always looks after her children.'

28

29

7

30

31

32

30 This image depicts the palm-wine pot that is never empty – the Asafo company is never lacking. (See also **40–1**)

31 The two animals represent the proverb, 'If the bush cow [or another herbivore] gets the bone it is for nothing, since it belongs to the dog.' (See also **203**)

32 The Asafo company is portrayed as the mother of the town. Here the implication is probably the same as that of the proverb, 'A good spirit always looks after her young.' (See also **17, 52**)

33

33 The figure carrying a two-pronged whip is an Asafo officer, accompanied by two soldiers, probably challenging a rival company.
34 'You say you are a man, but I have weighed your load and you are weak.'
35 This image is also about 'weighing' – assessing the strengths of – a rival company.

34

35

36

37

38

36 'Will you eat before you take an enema, or will you take an enema before you eat?' Both are excuses for failing to meet military responsibilities.

37, 38 Female Asafo officers confront small boys (rival companies), perhaps for stealing food.

36–8 are all examples of the late style – wide triangle borders and vivid colours.

39 The mythical giant Asebu Amanfi carries a barn full of corn, with his sister – in the window – frying the corn. He is often depicted using a cannon as a walking stick and with a palm-wine pot in his hand. Occasionally, he has multiple heads. (See also **19, 24**)

40, 41 Two flagmakers interpret the proverb, 'The palm-wine pot is never empty.' (See also **30**)

39

42 'The spider [Ananse] was on the stool before God made the earth.' The figure below the stool is from a popular print of Nebuchadnezzar on all fours.

43, 44 This image of a man holding up the world is a company boast of unlimited power and strength.

42

43

44

45, 46 A rare flag showing different images on each side. The identity of the tall, bearded, white-haired figure underneath a European crown is not known, but perhaps portrays an 'omanhen' – the paramount chief of the state.

47 The stool was the principal symbol of chieftaincy among the Akan, and this image implies that the company controls the state.

24

45

46

47

49

48 The white circle with animals, behind the red head, suggests a Christian halo or nimbus, perhaps indicating God's rule over nature.
49 'No one can defeat us except God.'

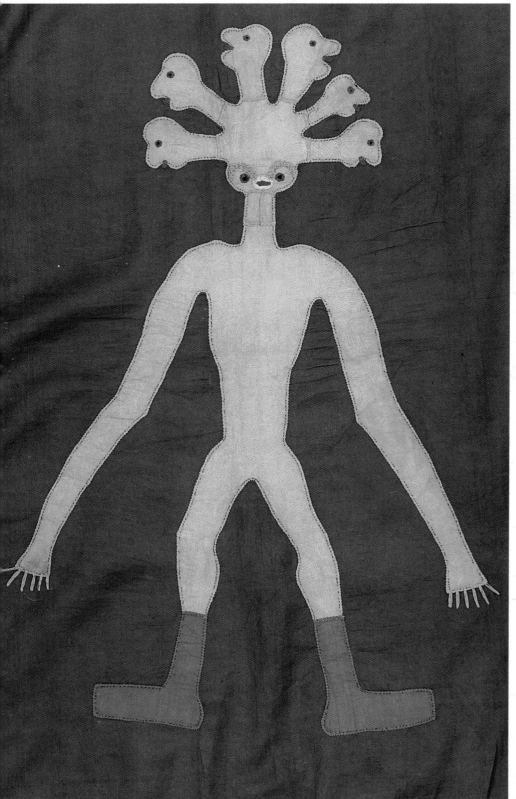

50 The mythical giant Asebu Amanfi is often depicted with multiple heads. (See also **19, 24**)

51 'Will you fly or will you vanish?' Either way, it is implied, you can't escape us. (See also **100, 107, 152, 154–6**)

52 'A good spirit always looks after her young.' A haunting image of Sasabansam or Funtum Yempa, a powerful and dangerous bush spirit that protects her friends and destroys their opponents. (See also **17**)

53

53 A drummer and three gong-gong beaters.
54 A group of captives. (See full flag, **197**)
55 An Asafo officer and three men, perhaps depicting, 'We come in peace but are prepared for war.' (See also **140** for a flag by the same flagmaker)
56 Perhaps an Asafo company dominating its larger but inferior rivals.

54

55

OVERLEAF
57 A captured opponent.
58 An ambush.
59 Confrontation.
60 'If our women are prepared for war, what will our men do?' If the women are this well armed, rival companies can expect the men to be invincible.

57

58

59

60

61

62

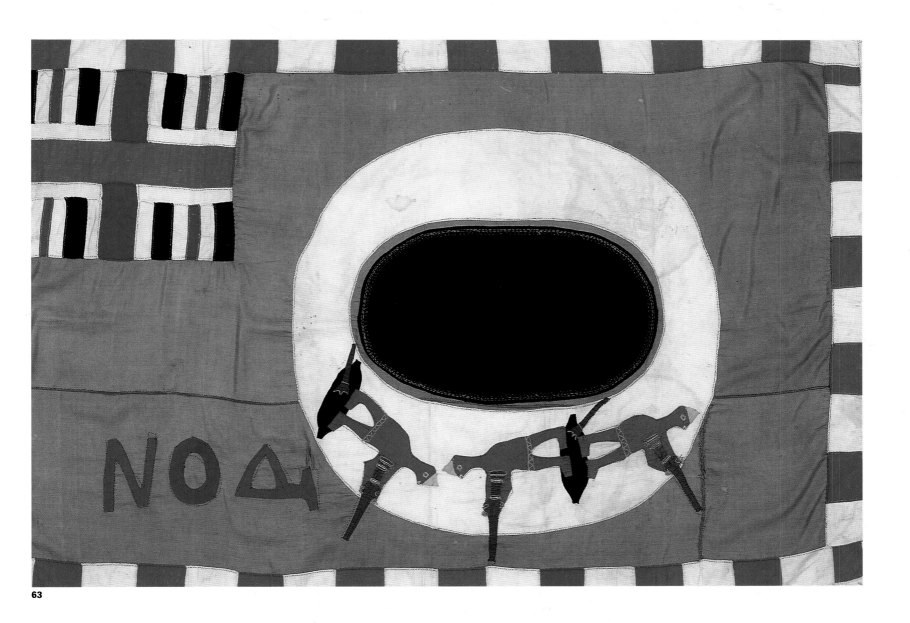

63

61 This flag probably recounts an historic incident in which rivals of the company were captured. (See also **67**)

62 Famous company victories in battle are portrayed in order to bolster company morale and to antagonize and intimidate the opposition. (See also **64–5, 201**)

63 Ponds or rivers with fish are often representations of specific gods that are acknowledged and protected by the Asafo company. (See also **114, 141**)

65

64 This flag either represents an historic confrontation between rival companies or depicts the company protecting a sacred pond. (See **63**)

65 A specific historic confrontation.

66 'Our enemies are like fish caught in a drag-net', that is, easily captured. (See also **116–17**)

67 The captured rivals. (See also **61**)

66

67

68

68 'We can defeat our rivals at draughts one thousand times a day.'
69 The draughtboard is a metaphor for war and is used to show the prowess of one company over another. (See also **91**)

69

70

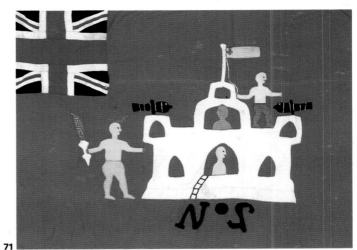

70, 71 Over thirty forts were built by the Europeans along the coast and were used in flag imagery as emblems of defensive strength. The company is boasting that it controls the fort, and therefore the town.
(See also **18, 171, 184**)

71

72

72, 73 Several proverbs relate to images of European ships: 'When a big ship is wrecked, everyone on board suffers.' (When calamity or defeat confronts the company, it touches everyone.) 'The ship is ready to sail.' 'The ship can carry a load of any size.' Five posubans – the companies' concrete shrines – were made in the shape of ships. (See also 20)

73

74, 75 'Like the aeroplane, we can go anywhere.'

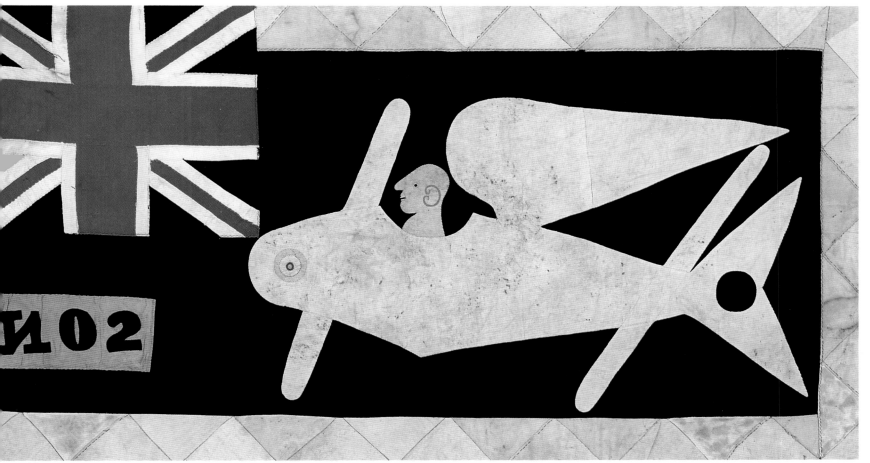

74

75

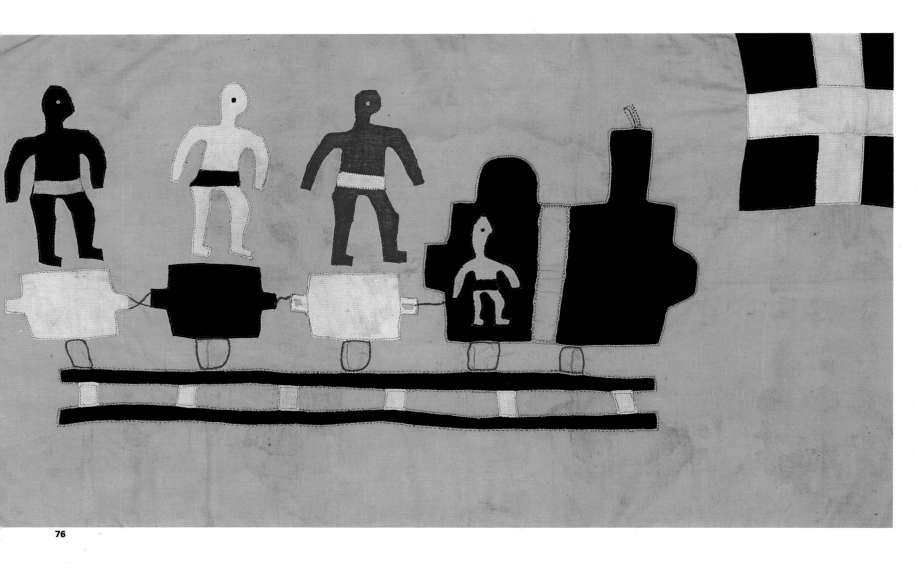

76

77

78

79

76, 77 'The train is always ready to go.' (See also 29). In 1903 a railroad from Sekondi to Kumasi was completed.

78, 79 Images of bridges almost always relate to controlling movements of peoples to and from town and are typical emblems of the company's power. The first motor car was brought to Ghana in 1901.

43

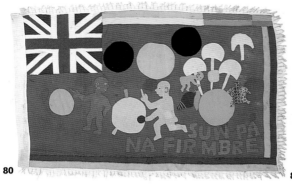

80

81

82

MAN AND NATURE

83

84

85

86 **87** **88**

In the often hostile world of the tropical forest abutting the Atlantic Ocean, the Fante have existed as a tribal unit since late medieval times, surviving as fishermen and farmers. Their everyday lives, therefore, are necessarily intimate with the natural world, as can be seen in the frequent flag imagery of animals, birds, insects, reptiles and fish, as well as the flora and fauna of the jungle.

Animals that portray strength include the elephant, bush-cow and whale. The leopard, eagle and crocodile are admired for their predatory powers, the porcupine for its arsenal of quills, the snake for its venom, the scorpion for its sting, the cockerel for its arrogance and the antelope for its intelligence. Rival companies are depicted as crows, vultures, mice, rats and fish.

The lion, a grasslands predator, is not found in the heavily forested ecology of the Fante, and almost certainly became a power symbol because of its frequent use in European heraldry. The lion was the quintessential visual metaphor for British power on the Gold Coast, adorning coats of arms, banners and company crests. On Asafo flags the great cat is usually depicted with its head turned to the side, wearing a crown, and in the

posture of the heraldic 'statant guardant' (148–51). The two-headed eagle, the most common bird in European heraldry, probably comes from the same source (106, 107, 181).

The palm tree, as already mentioned, was considered the strongest tree and symbol of eternity. The cactus and the pepper tree could be dangerous (157, 160, 163) and the Brebia vine, which covered even the tallest trees, impressed the Fante: 'Like the vine we can conquer any problem' (158, 164). Certain trees were considered sacred, and early company shrines were built around them. Three Fante flagmakers offer quite contrasting images of the guardian spirit of this tree (167–9).

Besides the two-headed eagle, another mythical monster is often depicted, again borrowing heavily from European heraldic images of dragons and griffins. This multi-headed, winged beast, with its fiercesome arsenal of weapons, was feared as an all-seeing, all-powerful and highly dangerous bush spirit. 'It can fly, it can dig in the ground, it can go anywhere.' The Fante also say: 'You think that this monster is going to do a bad thing, he thinks in secret that he is doing it. When you meet him, he will have done it' (154–6).

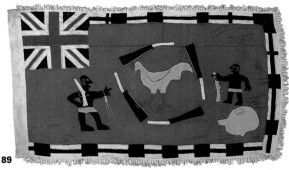

89 **90** **91**

92

92 Two proverbs apply: 'Without the head, the snake is nothing but rope'; and 'The white ant [termite] can conquer anything except the bottle'. Thus everyone has his match. The triangle represents an army of ants (the rival company), unable to eat the glass bottle (the company).

93 Again, two proverbs are relevant: 'Without the head, the snake is nothing but rope'; and 'If you put corn on the ground, birds will not be a rare sight'. (If you tempt or challenge us, you can expect a response.)

94 'A snake does not bite a man without cause.'

93

94

95 Possibly a highly stylized representation of the proverb, 'If the viper is too heavy to carry, why take the cobra as a head cushion.' (Don't bite off more than you can chew.)

95

96

97

96, 97 Two interpretations of 'We control the cock and the clock-bird' – we control time and decide when things are to be done. (Both birds announce the dawn with their cries.)

98 'Without the head, the snake is nothing but rope.' This proverb stresses the importance of leadership in the community.

99 Two birds in a tree, with a captive snake, may suggest strength in numbers, or may be a stylized 'heraldic' depiction of, 'Without the head, the snake is nothing but rope.'

99

98

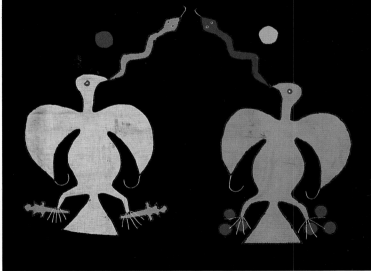

100

100 'Will you fly or will you vanish?' An unusual 'heraldic' representation of this proverb. (See also **51, 107, 152, 154–6**)

101 The hornbill borrowed money from the python and refused to repay the debt, figuring that the snake could never catch him. But the python was patient. One day a drought came. Eventually the hornbill had to land at the last remaining waterhole, where it was promptly caught by the patient python.

101

102

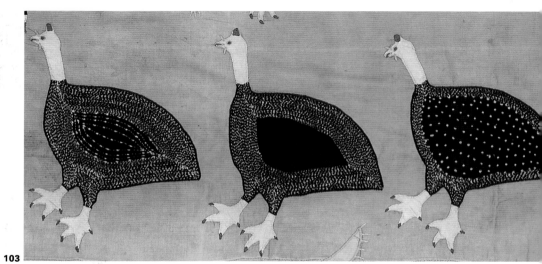

103

104

105

102 'We came to fight but not you mere vultures.' The Akan considered vultures to be unpleasant and offensive birds, thus providing a provocative metaphor for the opposition. (See also **196**)

103 Three guinea fowl.

104 'The crows and the vultures are playing draughts – who will win?' Both birds are metaphors for rival companies.

105 The image implies that the enemy can be defeated by birds.

106

106 'Even if you are an able hunter, never dare to hunt under the tree of an eagle.' The eagle is the most common bird in European heraldry and is often depicted with multiple heads, as are many Fante eagles.

107 'Will you fly or will you vanish?' and 'Without the head, the snake is nothing but rope'. Both proverbs apply.

107

108

109

108 The inspiration here may be the same proverb as 106.

109 'We are the lock and key of the state.' Locks, in the hands of Europeans, kept people in or out of an area, bringing freedom or slavery, and so their power was very real. This image is appliquéd, unusually, onto a traditional Ghanaian cloth.

110 The African grey parrot.

110

111

113

111 'When the eagle flies, it flies with its children' – there is strength in numbers. The blue face is a patch added later and is not part of the message.

112 'When there are no trees left, birds will perch on men's heads.' (Look for reasons behind the strange behaviour of others.)

113 'The big water bird swallows a fish from a different angle.' This suggests that the owners of the flag can accomplish things others find difficult.

112

114

114 Rivers with fish are often representations of specific gods that are acknowledged and protected by the Asafo company.

115 Perhaps the man is protecting the crop from scavenging birds (rival companies).

115

116, 117 'Our enemies are like fish caught in a drag-net.'

118 A beheaded fish. In flag imagery, fish usually imply rival companies.

119, 120 Catching fish symbolizes catching (defeating) the enemy.

116

117

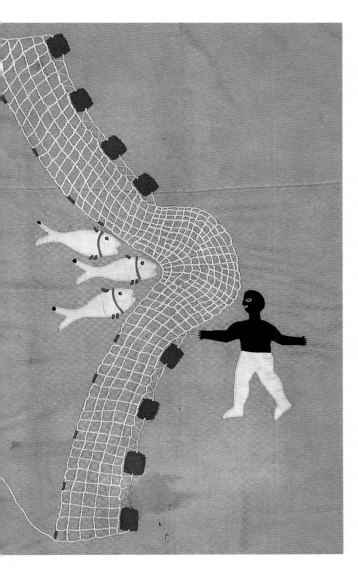

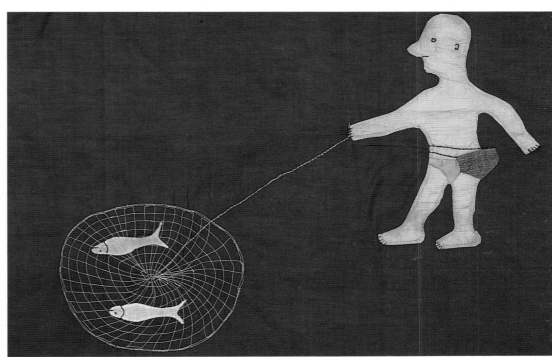

119

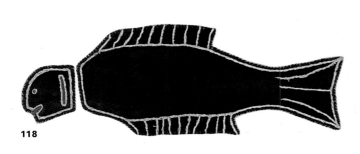

118

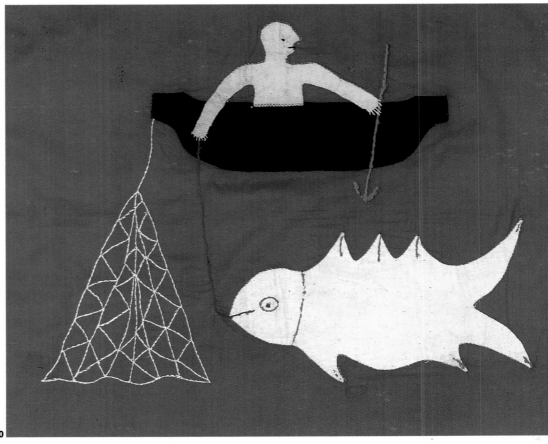

120

121

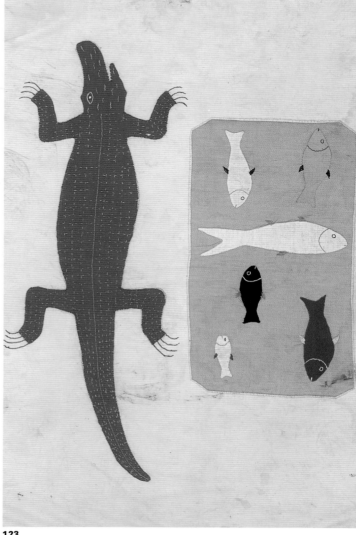

123

122

121, 122, 123 Three different interpretations of the proverb 'Fish grow fat for the benefit of the crocodile' (who rules the river). (See also **208**.) No. **121** is an early flag with a British printed ensign depicting King Edward VII (reigned 1901–10) and Queen Alexandra.

58

124 'The crab is feared for its claws', or 'The crab does not fear the rough sea'. In both instances the crab is seen as a fearless warrior.

59

125

126

127

125 The flag's owners are probably depicting themselves as cats and their opponents as mice.

126 'If the tree gets ripe, the birds will eat some fruit from it.'

127 This image probably implies that, just as the spider catches flies, so the company will trap its rivals.

128 'When the scorpion stings you, you must treat it in the same fashion' – fight fire with fire.

129 'We can carry water in a basket using a cactus as a cushion' – we can achieve the impossible.

130

131

132

130 'Only the lion drinks from the palm-wine pot of the leopard.'
131 The Asafo officer is standing over a gunpowder keg and facing a kneeling man with a goat: the meaning remains obscure.

132 'If you kill a thousand, a thousand will come.' The porcupine was considered to be an ideal warrior, able to shoot its spines at an enemy and then quickly to grow more to continue the fight.
133 Two other proverbs relate to this image: 'If you know how to hunt, it is not the porcupine you go after'; and 'If you play push with the porcupine, expect to get sore hands.'

133

134

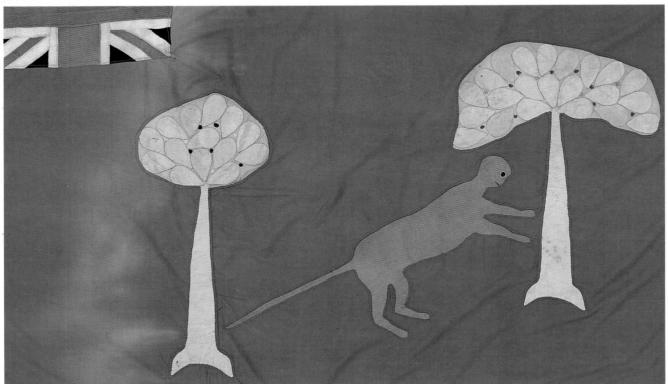

135

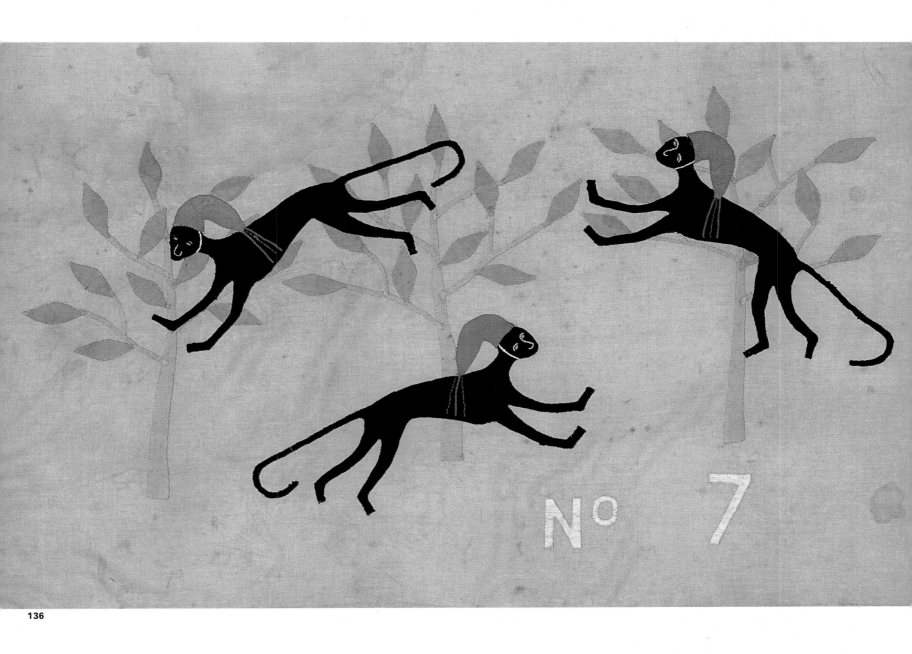

136

134, 135, 136 Three flagmakers visualize the proverb, 'The monkey leaps only as far as it can reach' – look before you leap. (See also **186**)

137

138

137 Two possible readings: either 'When the cat is dead the mice rejoice'; or 'The mice are even afraid of a dead cat.'
138 'It is a foolish mouse that steals from the bag of the cat.'

139 This image, a detail from the same flag as **47**, seems to be a boast that the company is so strong that it can carry both the state and an elephant.

140 'Although the elephant is stronger, we give the stool to the antelope.' A small company identifies with the wisdom of the antelope to counter its larger but inferior rival (the elephant) – brains before brawn.

139

140

141

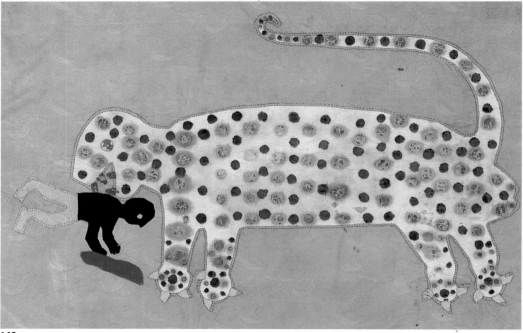

142

143

141 'Leopard' company guarding a sacred pond. (See also **63, 114**)

142 The leopard was a feared predator and a company emblem of power and strength.

143 Perhaps a depiction of the proverb, 'If you shoot at the leopard and do not kill it, it is better not to have shot at all.'

144 'Only a brave man will go under a big tree' – venture into the unknown. The posture and position of the two leopards shows the clear influence of European heraldry on the composition.

144

145

145 An embroidered lion.
146 Two possible interpretations. One salutes the incredible bravery of the Asafo company, the other derides the foolishness of the company's rival. In the first instance the flag's owners identify with the human figures, and in the second with the leopard.

147 'If you shoot at a leopard and do not kill it, it is better not to have shot at all.'

146

148

148 'The small boy does not know the lion' (otherwise he would not pull its tail). Besides belittling rivals as foolish 'small boys', this flag stresses the importance of education by showing the consequences of ignorance.

148, 149, 150, 151 The lion, a grasslands predator, is not found in the heavily forested ecology of the Fante coast, and its popularity as an emblem of power comes from its frequent use in European heraldry. The lion is nearly always depicted wearing a crown, with its tongue stuck out, and often in the posture of 'statant guardant'.

149

150

151

152

152 This image, adopted from Islam, represents al-Buraq, Muhammad's winged horse which carried the prophet on his nocturnal journey from Mecca to Jerusalem and then to the dome of the seven heavens. The image is used here as a version of the invincible flying monster that depicts the rhetorical question, 'Will you fly or will you vanish?' (See also **107, 153–6, 181**)

153 An unidentified monster sprouting snakes. A frightening mythological emblem of company power.

154–6 'Will you fly or will you vanish?' (Either way you can't escape us.) This image is inspired by the dragons, griffins, cockatrices and wyverns of European heraldry. The Fante say of this monster, 'It can fly, it can dig in the ground, it can go anywhere.'

153

154

155

156

157

157 'If a child wants to pick ripe pepper, let him do it. When it gets in his eyes, he will stop by himself.'

158 'Like the vine we can conquer any problem.' The Brebia vine, which covered even Ghana's tallest trees, impressed the Fante.

Three gong-gong beaters and an Asafo officer, characterized by his sword and pronged whip, also feature.

159 This image is a warning not to use a thorny branch or tree to wipe oneself after defecation.

158

159

160 Another interpretation of the child and the pepper, already seen in **157**.

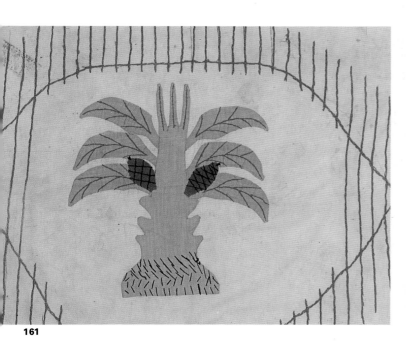

162

163

161 A pineapple tree. The cane fence around it suggests that it was also an Asafo shrine.
162 An unidentified, highly stylized blossoming plant or tree.
163 No. 1 Company, identifying with the cactus, warns rivals to keep their distance.

161

164

164 'Like the vine we can conquer any problem.' (See also **158, 166**)
165 Mother and child apparently trying to pick the last fruit off a sparse tree.
166 Both the porcupine and the Brebia vine are symbols of invincibility.

165

167

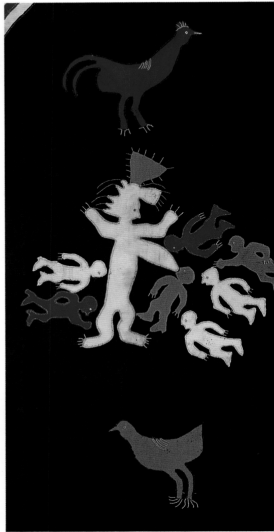

168

169

167–9 The original Asafo shrine was a tree with a cane fence around it ('dua ase') and a medicine mound ('etsiw'). Three flagmakers offer contrasting images of the female guardian spirit of this sacred tree.

170

171

172

FLAG STYLES AND FLAGMAKERS

173

174

175

177

178

A wide variety of styles, moods and techniques are evident in the corpus of pre-independence flags. The compositions grow from minimal to chaotic, the colours range from subtle to electric, the styles from primitive to classical, and the moods from grim to celebratory.

Determining the age of flags is made more difficult because flagmakers working in the same period, but in different areas, had quite contrasting approaches to composition and style, and many had pupils or 'schools' that faithfully copied the master in later periods. Nevertheless, the guiding factors would be the type of cloth, and its condition, the dyes used to colour the cloth, the mood and subject matter of the image, and the design and use of the borders.

From an examination of many flags, old and more recently made, it seems that there has been a distinct development over time in the style of the borders. The early flags show no borders at all and fringes are not in evidence. First borders are of thin continuous lines, or a series of rectangles. Later, triangles and fringes were introduced, and the border designs and the area of the flag devoted to the borders were enlarged, complete with a more lively use of colour. Some flagmakers

made certain border designs their own (96, 98, 155, 156, 177, 179, 180, 204–8). Borders on recently made flags tend to be loud and large, using electric colours that are stunning and effective, but that sometimes threaten to swamp the images within.

The obligatory Union Jack often receives liberal interpretations (23, 24, 28, 43, 87, 97, 125–7, 146). Whether these are simply artistic 'improvements', unfamiliarity with the original, or subtle digs at the British, the consistency in the style of these distortions by certain flagmakers effectively constitutes a signature (185–7; 188–90; 191–3; 194–6).

Their brief was to communicate graphically, in cloth, the commissioned proverbs, in a visual language that could be easily read and clearly understood. The eight flagmakers in the pages that follow each addressed that problem in very different ways. From the sparse, sinister images of 185–7 to the classical elegance of 204–8, they each display a confidence and an individuality of style. Their work, and that of the others in this book, gives some indication of the quality, breadth and depth of this extraordinary graphic movement – the flags of the Fante Asafo.

79

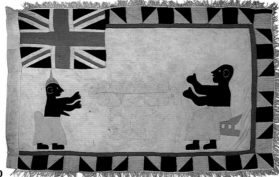

180

181

182 A bugler (detail of **184**).

183 The elephant with its trunk around a palm tree was a British symbol for the Gold Coast colony.

184 A representation of Cape Coast Castle, one of the forts built by the Europeans along the coast. The company is probably boasting that it controls the castle and therefore the town.

183

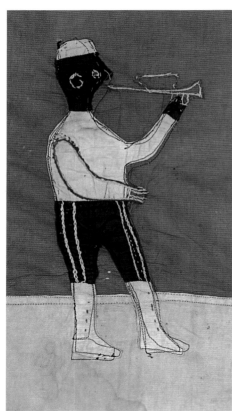

182

184

185

185 An Asafo company with a captured rival.

186 'The monkey leaps only as far as it can reach.' (See also **134–6**)

187 'If you set a trap maliciously, you might end up getting trapped yourself.' Other flags by this flagmaker or his 'school' are **77, 95, 108, 128, 165**.

186

187

188

188 The company is protecting its crop from scavengers (rivals).

189 An Asafo officer.

190 Perhaps 'Only a brave man will go under a big tree' (venture into the unknown).

Other flags by this flagmaker or his 'school' are **17, 43, 47, 57, 61, 63, 102, 106, 109, 139, 172**.

191, 192 The company captures and enslaves its enemies.

193 The female guardian spirit of the sacred tree. (See also **167**, which is a detail of this flag, and **168–9**)

190

189

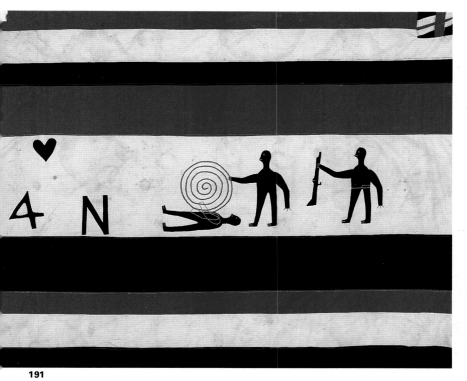

191

192

193

194 'Even if you are an able hunter, never dare hunt under the tree of an eagle.' (See also **106, 108**)

195 Rivals are depicted as animals 'playing' at Asafo.

196 The company mocks its rivals as mere vultures. (See also **102**)

Other flags by this flagmaker or his school are **27, 39, 66, 67, 68, 72, 99, 137, 171, 178** and **181**.

194

196

195

197 Captives are held by an Asafo officer.

198 Two proverbs are depicted: 'Even the elephant cannot uproot the palm tree'; and 'We can stand on ant hills and not be harmed.' Driver ants were feared for their destructive powers.

197

198

91

199

200

201

199 'Bellies mixed, crocodiles mixed, even though we have one stomach we fight over food, because food is for the mouth as much as for the stomach.' A metaphor arguing for community cooperation.

200 A complex image, which may relate to trade or to the harvest, but the precise meaning is unclear.

201 This flag probably depicts an historic confrontation between companies.

202

203

202 The image seems to imply that the company's rivals have no stomach for a fight.
203 'If the bush cow gets the bone, it is for nothing, since it belongs to the dog.' The bush cow does not eat meat. (See also **31**)
Other flags by this flagmaker or his school are
29, 35, 71, 103, 116, 134, 173–6.

204 Two proverbs: 'Only the elephant can uproot the palm tree'; and 'The hen may step on its chicks, but it does so to protect them not to harm them.'

205 'If all the rain falls and all the stars appear and shine, but the crab does not come out, no lagoon can empty its waters into the sea.'

206 An enigma – the star implies night (when the whale comes out), but the clock bird heralds dawn.

204

205

207 'Kwesie Inkoom' and 'Essiein Koomah' are the names of the two officers who commissioned this flag. The image probably relates to the power of the company.

208 'Fish grow fat for the benefit of the crocodile' (who rules the river).

Other flags by this flagmaker or his school are **14, 16, 26, 32, 74, 91, 96, 98, 132, 154, 155, 169, 170, 177, 179–80**.

This style of flag composition seems to have been the main influence for the late and post-independence flagmaking schools. (See **36–8, 49, 69, 75, 80, 86–8, 90, 111, 113–14, 124, 157, 160, 163**)

206

207

208

BIBLIOGRAPHY

209, 210 Details from a Fante Asafo shirt.

209 'Go back and fetch it.' The Sankofa bird, with its head turned back, emphasizes the value of learning from experience.
210 'We are the lock and key of the state.'

Acquah, G.A.
   1957 *The Fantes of Ghana*, Accra
Bowdich, Thomas Edward
   1819 *Mission from Cape Coast to Ashantee*, London
Casely Hayford, J.E.
   1903 *Gold Coast Native Institutions*, London
Christensen, James Boyd
   1954 *Double Descent Among the Fanti*, New Haven
   1958 'The Role of Proverbs in Fante Culture', *Africa* 28:232–43
Claridge, W. Walton
   1964 *A History of the Gold Coast and Ashanti*, London, 2 Vols
Cole, Herbert M. and Ross, Doran H.
   1977 *The Arts of Ghana*, Los Angeles
Cruikshank, Brodie
   1853 *Eighteen Years on the Gold Coast of Africa*, London, 2 Vols, reprinted 1966
Datta, Ansu K. and Porter, R.
   1972 'The Fante Asafo: A Re-examination', *Africa* 42:305–14
DeGraft Johnson, J.C.
   1932 'The Fanti Asafu', *Africa* 5:307–22
Ellis, Alfred Burden
   1887 *The Tshi-Speaking Peoples of the Gold Coast of West Africa*, London
ffoulkes, Arthur
   1907/08 'The Company System in Cape Coast Castle', *Journal of the African Society*, 7:261–77
Flynn, J.K.
   1971 *Asante and its Neighbours 1700–1807*, London
   1974–76 *Oral Traditions of the Fante States*, Legon, 7 Vols
Opoku, A.A.
   1970 *Festivals of Ghana*, Accra
Pedler, Frederick
   1974 *The Lion and the Unicorn in Africa*, London
Phillips, Thomas
   1752 'Journal of a Voyage Made in the Hannibal of London Ann.1693, 1694, from England . . . to Guinea', in Churchill's *Collection of Voyages and Travels*, London, Vol.VI
Porter, R.
   1970 'The Cape Coast Conflict of 1803', *Transactions of the Historical Society of Ghana*, xi:27–82
Preston, George Nelson
   1975 'Perseus and Medusa in Africa: Military Art in Fante-land 1834–1972', *African Arts*, 8(3):36–41, 68–71
Rattray, Robert
   1916 *Ashanti Proverbs*, Oxford
Ross, Doran H.
   1979 'Fighting with Art: Appliquéd Flags of the Fante Asafo', *UCLA Museum of Cultural History Pamphlet Series*, Vol.1, No.5
   1979 'Cement Lions and Cloth Elephants: Popular Arts of the Fante Asafo', in *Five Thousand Years of Popular Culture: Popular Culture before Printing*, Fred E.H. Schroeder (ed), for Bowling Green University Press
   1982 'The Heraldic Lion in Akan Art: A Study of Motif Assimilation in Southern Ghana', *Metropolitan Museum Journal*, 16
Sarbah, J. Mensah
   1897 *Fanti Customary Laws*, London
Smith, Whitney
   1975 *Flags Through the Ages and Across the World*, New York
Sutherland, D.A.
   1954 *State Emblems of the Gold Coast*, Accra
Thompson, Thomas
   1758 *An Account of Two Missionary Voyages*, London
Wartemberg, J.S.
   1951 *Sao Jorge D'El Mina*, Elms Court
Wolfson, Freda
   1958 *Pageant of Ghana*, London